50 Unique Dishes with Quinoa

By: Kelly Johnson

Table of Contents

- Quinoa and Black Bean Tacos
- Mediterranean Quinoa Salad
- Quinoa-Stuffed Peppers
- Quinoa and Chickpea Buddha Bowl
- Quinoa Breakfast Porridge
- Quinoa and Avocado Sushi Rolls
- Lemon Herb Quinoa Pilaf
- Quinoa and Kale Power Bowl
- Quinoa-Crusted Chicken Tenders
- Spicy Quinoa and Lentil Soup
- Quinoa and Roasted Veggie Wraps
- Thai Peanut Quinoa Bowl
- Quinoa and Shrimp Stir-Fry
- Quinoa-Stuffed Portobello Mushrooms
- Curried Quinoa and Cauliflower
- Quinoa and Turkey Meatballs
- Buffalo Quinoa Bites
- Quinoa and Mango Salad
- Teriyaki Quinoa and Tofu Bowl
- Quinoa and Roasted Beet Salad
- Quinoa and Cranberry Stuffing
- Quinoa Mac and Cheese
- Sweet Potato and Quinoa Hash
- Quinoa Falafel
- Quinoa and Black Bean Enchiladas
- Quinoa and Egg Breakfast Muffins
- Quinoa Veggie Burgers
- Quinoa-Stuffed Acorn Squash
- Sesame Ginger Quinoa Slaw
- Quinoa and Chocolate Protein Bars
- Quinoa and Spinach Frittata
- Quinoa and Pomegranate Salad
- Spiced Quinoa and Apple Breakfast Bowl
- Quinoa and Tomato Bruschetta
- Quinoa-Stuffed Cabbage Rolls

- Quinoa and Broccoli Casserole
- Quinoa and Roasted Garlic Hummus
- Blueberry Quinoa Pancakes
- BBQ Quinoa Sloppy Joes
- Coconut Quinoa Pudding
- Spicy Mexican Quinoa Skillet
- Quinoa and Chia Seed Pudding
- Cajun Quinoa Jambalaya
- Quinoa and Edamame Stir-Fry
- Quinoa and Zucchini Fritters
- Greek Quinoa Bowl with Feta
- Maple Cinnamon Quinoa Granola
- Miso Quinoa with Roasted Vegetables
- Quinoa and Pumpkin Seed Energy Bites
- Quinoa and Roasted Apple Crumble

Quinoa and Black Bean Tacos

Ingredients:

- 1 cup quinoa, cooked
- 1 can (400g) black beans, drained and rinsed
- 1 tbsp olive oil
- 1 tsp cumin
- 1 tsp chili powder
- 1/2 tsp paprika
- Salt and pepper to taste
- 8 small taco shells
- 1 cup shredded lettuce
- 1 tomato, diced
- 1/2 cup shredded cheese (optional)
- Salsa and sour cream for serving

Instructions:

1. Heat olive oil in a skillet over medium heat.
2. Add quinoa, black beans, cumin, chili powder, paprika, salt, and pepper. Stir well and cook for 5 minutes.
3. Warm taco shells and fill with quinoa mixture.
4. Top with lettuce, tomato, cheese, salsa, and sour cream.

Mediterranean Quinoa Salad

Ingredients:

- 1 cup quinoa, cooked and cooled
- 1/2 cucumber, diced
- 1/2 cup cherry tomatoes, halved
- 1/4 cup red onion, diced
- 1/4 cup kalamata olives, sliced
- 1/4 cup feta cheese, crumbled
- 2 tbsp olive oil
- 1 tbsp lemon juice
- 1 tsp oregano
- Salt and pepper to taste

Instructions:

1. In a large bowl, combine quinoa, cucumber, tomatoes, red onion, olives, and feta.
2. Drizzle with olive oil and lemon juice.
3. Sprinkle with oregano, salt, and pepper. Toss to combine and serve chilled.

Quinoa-Stuffed Peppers

Ingredients:

- 4 bell peppers, tops cut off and seeds removed
- 1 cup quinoa, cooked
- 1/2 cup black beans
- 1/2 cup corn
- 1/2 cup diced tomatoes
- 1/2 tsp cumin
- 1/2 tsp chili powder
- 1/2 cup shredded cheese (optional)
- Salt and pepper to taste

Instructions:

1. Preheat the oven to 180°C (350°F).
2. Mix quinoa, black beans, corn, tomatoes, cumin, chili powder, salt, and pepper in a bowl.
3. Stuff each bell pepper with the quinoa mixture.
4. Top with cheese if using, then bake for 25-30 minutes until the peppers are tender.

Quinoa and Chickpea Buddha Bowl

Ingredients:

- 1 cup quinoa, cooked
- 1/2 cup chickpeas, drained and rinsed
- 1/2 avocado, sliced
- 1/2 cup roasted sweet potatoes
- 1/2 cup steamed broccoli
- 1 tbsp tahini
- 1 tbsp lemon juice
- Salt and pepper to taste

Instructions:

1. Arrange quinoa, chickpeas, avocado, sweet potatoes, and broccoli in a bowl.
2. Drizzle with tahini and lemon juice.
3. Season with salt and pepper and serve.

Quinoa Breakfast Porridge

Ingredients:

- 1/2 cup quinoa, rinsed
- 1 cup almond milk (or any milk)
- 1 tbsp maple syrup or honey
- 1/2 tsp cinnamon
- 1/4 cup fresh berries
- 1 tbsp nuts or seeds

Instructions:

1. Cook quinoa with almond milk over medium heat until tender (about 15 minutes).
2. Stir in maple syrup and cinnamon.
3. Top with fresh berries and nuts before serving.

Quinoa and Avocado Sushi Rolls

Ingredients:

- 1 cup quinoa, cooked and cooled
- 1 tbsp rice vinegar
- 4 nori sheets
- 1/2 avocado, sliced
- 1/2 cucumber, julienned
- 1/2 carrot, julienned
- Soy sauce for dipping

Instructions:

1. Mix quinoa with rice vinegar.
2. Lay a nori sheet on a sushi mat and spread a thin layer of quinoa on it.
3. Arrange avocado, cucumber, and carrot in a line.
4. Roll tightly, slice, and serve with soy sauce.

Lemon Herb Quinoa Pilaf

Ingredients:

- 1 cup quinoa, cooked
- 1 tbsp olive oil
- 1 clove garlic, minced
- 1/2 cup chopped parsley
- 1 tbsp lemon juice
- 1 tsp lemon zest
- Salt and pepper to taste

Instructions:

1. Heat olive oil in a pan and sauté garlic until fragrant.
2. Stir in cooked quinoa, parsley, lemon juice, and lemon zest.
3. Season with salt and pepper and serve warm.

Quinoa and Kale Power Bowl

Ingredients:

- 1 cup quinoa, cooked
- 1 cup kale, chopped
- 1/2 cup roasted chickpeas
- 1/2 cup shredded carrots
- 1/2 avocado, sliced
- 2 tbsp hummus
- 1 tbsp lemon juice

Instructions:

1. Massage kale with lemon juice for 2 minutes until softened.
2. Arrange quinoa, kale, chickpeas, carrots, and avocado in a bowl.
3. Top with hummus and serve.

Quinoa-Crusted Chicken Tenders

Ingredients:

- 2 chicken breasts, cut into strips
- 1/2 cup cooked quinoa
- 1/2 cup breadcrumbs
- 1 egg, beaten
- 1 tsp garlic powder
- 1/2 tsp salt
- 1/2 tsp black pepper

Instructions:

1. Preheat the oven to 200°C (400°F).
2. Mix quinoa, breadcrumbs, garlic powder, salt, and pepper.
3. Dip chicken strips in beaten egg, then coat with quinoa mixture.
4. Place on a baking sheet and bake for 20-25 minutes until crispy.

Spicy Quinoa and Lentil Soup

Ingredients:

- 1 cup quinoa, rinsed
- 1/2 cup red lentils
- 1 onion, chopped
- 2 cloves garlic, minced
- 1 can (400g) diced tomatoes
- 4 cups vegetable broth
- 1 tsp cumin
- 1 tsp smoked paprika
- 1/2 tsp cayenne pepper
- Salt and pepper to taste
- 1 tbsp olive oil

Instructions:

1. Heat olive oil in a pot and sauté onion and garlic until soft.
2. Add quinoa, lentils, diced tomatoes, vegetable broth, cumin, paprika, cayenne, salt, and pepper.
3. Bring to a boil, then reduce heat and simmer for 25-30 minutes until lentils are soft.
4. Serve hot with fresh herbs or a squeeze of lemon juice.

Quinoa and Roasted Veggie Wraps

Ingredients:

- 1 cup quinoa, cooked
- 1 zucchini, sliced
- 1 red bell pepper, sliced
- 1 cup cherry tomatoes, halved
- 1/2 red onion, sliced
- 1 tbsp olive oil
- 1 tsp garlic powder
- Salt and pepper to taste
- 4 whole wheat wraps
- 1/2 cup hummus

Instructions:

1. Preheat the oven to 200°C (400°F).
2. Toss zucchini, bell pepper, tomatoes, and onion with olive oil, garlic powder, salt, and pepper. Roast for 20 minutes.
3. Spread hummus on each wrap, then add cooked quinoa and roasted veggies.
4. Roll up the wraps tightly and serve.

Thai Peanut Quinoa Bowl

Ingredients:

- 1 cup quinoa, cooked
- 1/2 cup shredded carrots
- 1/2 cup red bell pepper, sliced
- 1/2 cup edamame
- 1/4 cup chopped peanuts
- 2 tbsp chopped cilantro
- 2 tbsp peanut butter
- 1 tbsp soy sauce
- 1 tsp sesame oil
- 1 tsp lime juice

Instructions:

1. Whisk together peanut butter, soy sauce, sesame oil, and lime juice.
2. In a bowl, mix quinoa, carrots, bell pepper, edamame, and cilantro.
3. Drizzle with peanut sauce and toss to combine.
4. Top with chopped peanuts and serve.

Quinoa and Shrimp Stir-Fry

Ingredients:

- 1 cup quinoa, cooked
- 250g shrimp, peeled and deveined
- 1 tbsp soy sauce
- 1 tbsp olive oil
- 1/2 cup bell peppers, sliced
- 1/2 cup snow peas
- 2 cloves garlic, minced
- 1/2 tsp ginger, grated

Instructions:

1. Heat olive oil in a skillet and cook shrimp for 2-3 minutes per side. Remove and set aside.
2. Add bell peppers, snow peas, garlic, and ginger to the pan. Sauté for 3 minutes.
3. Stir in cooked quinoa and soy sauce, then add shrimp back to the pan.
4. Toss to combine and serve.

Quinoa-Stuffed Portobello Mushrooms

Ingredients:

- 4 large Portobello mushrooms, stems removed
- 1 cup quinoa, cooked
- 1/2 cup spinach, chopped
- 1/2 cup cherry tomatoes, diced
- 1/4 cup feta cheese, crumbled
- 1 tbsp olive oil
- 1 tsp oregano
- Salt and pepper to taste

Instructions:

1. Preheat the oven to 200°C (400°F).
2. Brush mushrooms with olive oil and place on a baking sheet.
3. Mix quinoa, spinach, tomatoes, feta, oregano, salt, and pepper.
4. Stuff the mushrooms with the quinoa mixture.
5. Bake for 15-20 minutes until mushrooms are tender.

Curried Quinoa and Cauliflower

Ingredients:

- 1 cup quinoa, cooked
- 1 cup cauliflower florets
- 1/2 onion, chopped
- 1 tbsp curry powder
- 1/2 tsp turmeric
- 1/2 tsp cumin
- 1/2 tsp salt
- 1 tbsp coconut oil
- 1/4 cup coconut milk

Instructions:

1. Heat coconut oil in a pan and sauté onion until soft.
2. Add cauliflower, curry powder, turmeric, cumin, and salt. Cook for 5 minutes.
3. Stir in cooked quinoa and coconut milk. Simmer for 5 minutes until combined.
4. Serve warm with fresh cilantro.

Quinoa and Turkey Meatballs

Ingredients:

- 500g ground turkey
- 1/2 cup cooked quinoa
- 1 egg
- 1/4 cup Parmesan cheese, grated
- 1 tsp garlic powder
- 1 tsp oregano
- Salt and pepper to taste

Instructions:

1. Preheat the oven to 200°C (400°F).
2. Mix all ingredients in a bowl and form into small meatballs.
3. Place on a baking sheet and bake for 20 minutes, flipping halfway through.
4. Serve with marinara sauce or over pasta.

Buffalo Quinoa Bites

Ingredients:

- 1 cup quinoa, cooked
- 1/2 cup shredded cheddar cheese
- 1/2 cup cooked shredded chicken
- 1 egg
- 2 tbsp buffalo sauce
- 1/2 tsp garlic powder

Instructions:

1. Preheat the oven to 200°C (400°F).
2. Mix all ingredients in a bowl.
3. Form small bites and place on a lined baking sheet.
4. Bake for 15-20 minutes until golden and crispy.
5. Serve with ranch or blue cheese dressing.

Quinoa and Mango Salad

Ingredients:

- 1 cup quinoa, cooked and cooled
- 1 ripe mango, diced
- 1/2 red bell pepper, diced
- 1/4 cup red onion, diced
- 1/4 cup fresh cilantro, chopped
- 2 tbsp lime juice
- 1 tbsp olive oil
- Salt and pepper to taste

Instructions:

1. In a large bowl, combine quinoa, mango, bell pepper, red onion, and cilantro.
2. Whisk together lime juice, olive oil, salt, and pepper, then pour over the salad.
3. Toss to combine and serve chilled.

Teriyaki Quinoa and Tofu Bowl

Ingredients:

- 1 cup quinoa, cooked
- 1 block firm tofu, cubed
- 1/4 cup teriyaki sauce
- 1/2 cup broccoli florets
- 1/2 cup shredded carrots
- 1/4 cup edamame
- 1 tbsp sesame oil
- 1 tbsp sesame seeds

Instructions:

1. Marinate tofu in teriyaki sauce for 15 minutes.
2. Heat sesame oil in a pan and sauté tofu until golden brown.
3. Add broccoli, carrots, and edamame, and cook for 3-5 minutes.
4. Stir in cooked quinoa and remaining teriyaki sauce.
5. Garnish with sesame seeds and serve.

Quinoa and Roasted Beet Salad

Ingredients:

- 1 cup quinoa, cooked and cooled
- 2 medium beets, roasted and diced
- 1/4 cup goat cheese, crumbled
- 1/4 cup walnuts, chopped
- 2 tbsp balsamic vinegar
- 1 tbsp olive oil
- 1 tsp honey
- Salt and pepper to taste

Instructions:

1. Roast beets at 200°C (400°F) for 40-50 minutes, then dice.
2. In a bowl, combine quinoa, beets, goat cheese, and walnuts.
3. Whisk balsamic vinegar, olive oil, honey, salt, and pepper together and drizzle over salad.
4. Toss and serve.

Quinoa and Cranberry Stuffing

Ingredients:

- 1 cup quinoa, cooked
- 1/2 cup dried cranberries
- 1/2 cup celery, diced
- 1/2 cup onion, diced
- 1/4 cup pecans, chopped
- 1 tsp sage
- 1 tsp thyme
- 1 tbsp olive oil
- Salt and pepper to taste

Instructions:

1. Heat olive oil in a pan and sauté onion and celery until soft.
2. Stir in quinoa, cranberries, pecans, sage, thyme, salt, and pepper.
3. Serve as a side dish or stuffing alternative.

Quinoa Mac and Cheese

Ingredients:

- 2 cups quinoa, cooked
- 1 cup milk
- 1 cup shredded cheddar cheese
- 1/2 cup Parmesan cheese, grated
- 1 tbsp butter
- 1/2 tsp garlic powder
- Salt and pepper to taste

Instructions:

1. In a saucepan, heat milk, butter, garlic powder, salt, and pepper.
2. Stir in cheddar and Parmesan cheese until melted.
3. Mix in cooked quinoa and stir until combined.
4. Serve warm.

Sweet Potato and Quinoa Hash

Ingredients:

- 1 cup quinoa, cooked
- 1 medium sweet potato, diced
- 1/2 onion, chopped
- 1/2 red bell pepper, chopped
- 1 clove garlic, minced
- 1 tbsp olive oil
- 1/2 tsp smoked paprika
- Salt and pepper to taste

Instructions:

1. Heat olive oil in a skillet and sauté sweet potato for 5-7 minutes.
2. Add onion, bell pepper, and garlic, cooking until soft.
3. Stir in quinoa, paprika, salt, and pepper.
4. Serve warm, optionally topped with a fried egg.

Quinoa Falafel

Ingredients:

- 1 cup quinoa, cooked
- 1 can (400g) chickpeas, drained
- 1/4 cup parsley, chopped
- 2 cloves garlic, minced
- 1 tsp cumin
- 1 tsp coriander
- 2 tbsp flour
- 1 tbsp lemon juice
- Salt and pepper to taste
- Oil for frying

Instructions:

1. Blend chickpeas, quinoa, parsley, garlic, cumin, coriander, flour, lemon juice, salt, and pepper in a food processor until combined.
2. Form into small patties.
3. Fry in a pan with oil for 2-3 minutes per side until golden brown.
4. Serve with hummus or tzatziki.

Quinoa and Black Bean Enchiladas

Ingredients:

- 1 cup quinoa, cooked
- 1 can (400g) black beans, drained
- 1/2 cup corn
- 1/2 cup shredded cheese
- 1/2 tsp cumin
- 1/2 tsp chili powder
- 6 corn tortillas
- 1 cup enchilada sauce

Instructions:

1. Preheat oven to 180°C (350°F).
2. Mix quinoa, black beans, corn, cheese, cumin, and chili powder in a bowl.
3. Fill tortillas with the mixture and roll tightly.
4. Place in a baking dish, top with enchilada sauce and extra cheese.
5. Bake for 20 minutes and serve.

Quinoa and Egg Breakfast Muffins

Ingredients:

- 1 cup quinoa, cooked
- 6 eggs
- 1/2 cup spinach, chopped
- 1/2 cup bell pepper, diced
- 1/4 cup feta cheese, crumbled
- Salt and pepper to taste

Instructions:

1. Preheat oven to 180°C (350°F) and grease a muffin tin.
2. Whisk eggs, then mix in quinoa, spinach, bell pepper, feta, salt, and pepper.
3. Pour mixture into muffin tins, filling 3/4 full.
4. Bake for 15-20 minutes until set.

Quinoa Veggie Burgers

Ingredients:

- 1 cup quinoa, cooked
- 1 can (400g) black beans, drained
- 1/2 cup breadcrumbs
- 1/2 onion, finely chopped
- 1 tsp garlic powder
- 1 tsp cumin
- 1 egg
- Salt and pepper to taste

Instructions:

1. Mash black beans in a bowl.
2. Stir in quinoa, breadcrumbs, onion, garlic powder, cumin, egg, salt, and pepper.
3. Form into burger patties.
4. Cook in a pan with oil for 3-4 minutes per side.
5. Serve on buns with toppings of choice.

Quinoa-Stuffed Acorn Squash

Ingredients:

- 2 acorn squash, halved and seeded
- 1 cup quinoa, cooked
- 1/2 cup dried cranberries
- 1/4 cup pecans, chopped
- 1/2 tsp cinnamon
- 1/2 tsp nutmeg
- Salt and pepper to taste
- 2 tbsp maple syrup

Instructions:

1. Preheat oven to 200°C (400°F).
2. Brush acorn squash halves with olive oil, season with salt and pepper, and place cut side down on a baking sheet. Roast for 25-30 minutes until tender.
3. In a bowl, combine cooked quinoa, cranberries, pecans, cinnamon, nutmeg, and maple syrup.
4. Stuff the roasted squash halves with the quinoa mixture and bake for another 10 minutes.

Sesame Ginger Quinoa Slaw

Ingredients:

- 1 cup quinoa, cooked
- 1 1/2 cups shredded cabbage
- 1 carrot, shredded
- 1/4 cup green onions, chopped
- 2 tbsp sesame oil
- 1 tbsp soy sauce
- 1 tbsp rice vinegar
- 1 tsp grated ginger
- 1 tsp sesame seeds

Instructions:

1. In a large bowl, combine quinoa, cabbage, carrot, and green onions.
2. In a small bowl, whisk together sesame oil, soy sauce, rice vinegar, and ginger.
3. Pour dressing over quinoa mixture and toss to combine.
4. Sprinkle with sesame seeds and serve chilled.

Quinoa and Chocolate Protein Bars

Ingredients:

- 1 cup quinoa, cooked and cooled
- 1/2 cup peanut butter
- 1/4 cup honey
- 1/2 cup chocolate protein powder
- 1/4 cup cocoa powder
- 1/4 cup dark chocolate chips (optional)
- 1/2 tsp vanilla extract

Instructions:

1. In a bowl, mix quinoa, peanut butter, honey, protein powder, cocoa powder, and vanilla.
2. Press the mixture into a baking dish lined with parchment paper.
3. Refrigerate for 1-2 hours until firm.
4. Cut into bars and store in an airtight container.

Quinoa and Spinach Frittata

Ingredients:

- 1 cup quinoa, cooked
- 4 eggs
- 1/2 cup milk
- 1/2 onion, chopped
- 1 cup spinach, chopped
- 1/4 cup feta cheese, crumbled
- Salt and pepper to taste

Instructions:

1. Preheat the oven to 180°C (350°F).
2. In a skillet, sauté onion until soft. Add spinach and cook until wilted.
3. In a bowl, whisk eggs, milk, salt, and pepper. Stir in cooked quinoa and feta.
4. Pour the egg mixture into the skillet with spinach and onions.
5. Bake for 20-25 minutes until set and golden.

Quinoa and Pomegranate Salad

Ingredients:

- 1 cup quinoa, cooked
- 1/2 cup pomegranate seeds
- 1 cucumber, diced
- 1/4 cup red onion, diced
- 1/4 cup fresh mint, chopped
- 2 tbsp olive oil
- 1 tbsp lemon juice
- Salt and pepper to taste

Instructions:

1. In a large bowl, combine quinoa, pomegranate seeds, cucumber, red onion, and mint.
2. Drizzle with olive oil and lemon juice, and season with salt and pepper.
3. Toss to combine and serve chilled.

Spiced Quinoa and Apple Breakfast Bowl

Ingredients:

- 1 cup quinoa, cooked
- 1 apple, diced
- 1/4 tsp cinnamon
- 1 tbsp maple syrup
- 1/4 cup chopped walnuts
- 1/4 cup almond milk or dairy milk

Instructions:

1. In a bowl, combine cooked quinoa, diced apple, cinnamon, and maple syrup.
2. Heat in the microwave or on the stove with almond milk until warm.
3. Top with chopped walnuts and serve.

Quinoa and Tomato Bruschetta

Ingredients:

- 1 cup quinoa, cooked
- 1 pint cherry tomatoes, halved
- 1/4 cup fresh basil, chopped
- 2 tbsp balsamic vinegar
- 1 tbsp olive oil
- Salt and pepper to taste
- 1 loaf baguette, sliced and toasted

Instructions:

1. In a bowl, combine quinoa, cherry tomatoes, basil, balsamic vinegar, and olive oil.
2. Season with salt and pepper.
3. Spoon the quinoa mixture onto toasted baguette slices and serve immediately.

Quinoa-Stuffed Cabbage Rolls

Ingredients:

- 8 large cabbage leaves
- 1 cup quinoa, cooked
- 1/2 cup cooked ground beef or turkey
- 1/2 cup onion, chopped
- 1/4 cup parsley, chopped
- 1 cup tomato sauce
- 1 tsp paprika
- Salt and pepper to taste

Instructions:

1. Preheat the oven to 180°C (350°F).
2. Blanch cabbage leaves in boiling water for 2 minutes to soften.
3. Mix quinoa, ground meat, onion, parsley, paprika, salt, and pepper.
4. Spoon mixture onto cabbage leaves and roll them up tightly.
5. Place rolls in a baking dish, cover with tomato sauce, and bake for 30 minutes.

Quinoa and Broccoli Casserole

Ingredients:

- 1 cup quinoa, cooked
- 2 cups broccoli florets, steamed
- 1/2 cup cheddar cheese, shredded
- 1/2 cup Greek yogurt
- 1/4 cup milk
- 1 tsp garlic powder
- Salt and pepper to taste

Instructions:

1. Preheat the oven to 180°C (350°F).
2. In a bowl, mix quinoa, broccoli, cheese, Greek yogurt, milk, garlic powder, salt, and pepper.
3. Pour into a greased baking dish and bake for 20-25 minutes until golden and bubbly.
4. Serve as a side dish or light main course.

Quinoa and Roasted Garlic Hummus

Ingredients:

- 1 cup quinoa, cooked
- 1 cup canned chickpeas, drained
- 1 head garlic, roasted
- 2 tbsp tahini
- 2 tbsp lemon juice
- 2 tbsp olive oil
- 1/2 tsp cumin
- Salt and pepper to taste

Instructions:

1. Preheat the oven to 180°C (350°F).
2. Slice the top off the garlic head, drizzle with olive oil, and roast for 30 minutes until soft.
3. In a food processor, combine quinoa, chickpeas, roasted garlic (squeeze out the cloves), tahini, lemon juice, cumin, salt, and pepper.
4. Blend until smooth, adding olive oil or water for desired consistency.
5. Serve with veggies or pita bread.

Blueberry Quinoa Pancakes

Ingredients:

- 1 cup quinoa flour (or cooked quinoa)
- 1/2 cup all-purpose flour
- 2 tbsp sugar
- 1 tbsp baking powder
- 1/4 tsp salt
- 1 cup milk (or almond milk)
- 1 egg
- 1 tsp vanilla extract
- 1/2 cup fresh or frozen blueberries
- Butter or oil for cooking

Instructions:

1. In a bowl, whisk together quinoa flour, all-purpose flour, sugar, baking powder, and salt.
2. In another bowl, whisk together milk, egg, and vanilla.
3. Pour the wet ingredients into the dry and mix until combined.
4. Fold in blueberries.
5. Heat a skillet over medium heat, add a little butter or oil, and cook pancakes for 2-3 minutes on each side until golden brown.

BBQ Quinoa Sloppy Joes

Ingredients:

- 1 cup quinoa, cooked
- 1 can (400g) lentils, drained
- 1/2 cup BBQ sauce
- 1/2 onion, chopped
- 1 bell pepper, chopped
- 1 tbsp olive oil
- 4 whole-wheat buns
- Salt and pepper to taste

Instructions:

1. Heat olive oil in a pan and sauté onion and bell pepper until soft.
2. Stir in cooked quinoa and lentils, cooking for 3-4 minutes.
3. Add BBQ sauce, salt, and pepper, and cook for an additional 5 minutes until heated through.
4. Spoon the mixture onto buns and serve immediately.

Coconut Quinoa Pudding

Ingredients:

- 1 cup quinoa, cooked
- 1 can (400g) coconut milk
- 2 tbsp maple syrup
- 1/2 tsp vanilla extract
- 1/4 tsp cinnamon
- Fresh berries for topping (optional)

Instructions:

1. In a saucepan, combine cooked quinoa, coconut milk, maple syrup, vanilla, and cinnamon.
2. Bring to a simmer over medium heat and cook for 10-12 minutes until thickened.
3. Serve warm or chilled, topped with fresh berries.

Spicy Mexican Quinoa Skillet

Ingredients:

- 1 cup quinoa, cooked
- 1 can (400g) black beans, drained
- 1 cup corn kernels (fresh or frozen)
- 1 tsp cumin
- 1 tsp chili powder
- 1/2 tsp paprika
- 1/4 tsp cayenne pepper
- 1/2 onion, chopped
- 1 tbsp olive oil
- 1/4 cup fresh cilantro, chopped
- 1/2 cup shredded cheese (optional)

Instructions:

1. Heat olive oil in a large skillet and sauté onions for 3-4 minutes.
2. Add cumin, chili powder, paprika, and cayenne, cooking for another minute.
3. Stir in quinoa, black beans, and corn, and cook for 5-7 minutes until heated through.
4. Top with cilantro and cheese (optional), and serve.

Quinoa and Chia Seed Pudding

Ingredients:

- 1/2 cup quinoa, cooked
- 1/4 cup chia seeds
- 1 1/2 cups almond milk (or milk of choice)
- 2 tbsp honey or maple syrup
- 1 tsp vanilla extract
- Fresh fruit for topping

Instructions:

1. In a bowl, combine cooked quinoa, chia seeds, almond milk, honey, and vanilla extract.
2. Stir well, cover, and refrigerate for at least 4 hours or overnight to thicken.
3. Top with fresh fruit and serve.

Cajun Quinoa Jambalaya

Ingredients:

- 1 cup quinoa, cooked
- 1/2 lb sausage (chicken, turkey, or vegetarian)
- 1 bell pepper, chopped
- 1 celery stalk, chopped
- 1 onion, chopped
- 2 cloves garlic, minced
- 1 can (400g) diced tomatoes
- 1 tsp smoked paprika
- 1/2 tsp cayenne pepper
- 1/2 tsp thyme
- 1/4 tsp oregano
- 1 tbsp olive oil
- Salt and pepper to taste

Instructions:

1. In a large pan, heat olive oil and sauté sausage, bell pepper, celery, onion, and garlic until softened.
2. Stir in diced tomatoes, smoked paprika, cayenne, thyme, oregano, quinoa, salt, and pepper.
3. Add a little water if needed, and simmer for 10 minutes.
4. Serve hot with fresh parsley or scallions on top.

Quinoa and Edamame Stir-Fry

Ingredients:

- 1 cup quinoa, cooked
- 1 cup edamame, shelled
- 1/2 bell pepper, sliced
- 1/2 onion, chopped
- 2 cloves garlic, minced
- 1 tbsp soy sauce
- 1 tbsp sesame oil
- 1/2 tsp ginger, grated
- 1 tbsp sesame seeds (optional)
- Salt and pepper to taste

Instructions:

1. Heat sesame oil in a large pan over medium heat. Add garlic, onion, and bell pepper, sautéing for 3-4 minutes until soft.
2. Stir in edamame, cooked quinoa, soy sauce, ginger, and salt. Cook for another 5 minutes, stirring occasionally.
3. Sprinkle with sesame seeds before serving. Serve hot.

Quinoa and Zucchini Fritters

Ingredients:

- 1 cup quinoa, cooked
- 2 medium zucchinis, grated
- 1/4 cup flour (all-purpose or chickpea)
- 1 egg
- 2 tbsp Parmesan cheese, grated
- 1 tbsp fresh parsley, chopped
- 1/2 tsp garlic powder
- Salt and pepper to taste
- Olive oil for frying

Instructions:

1. In a large bowl, combine grated zucchini, cooked quinoa, flour, egg, Parmesan, parsley, garlic powder, salt, and pepper.
2. Heat olive oil in a skillet over medium heat.
3. Scoop spoonfuls of the mixture into the pan and flatten slightly. Cook for 3-4 minutes on each side until golden and crispy.
4. Serve with a dollop of yogurt or your favorite dipping sauce.

Greek Quinoa Bowl with Feta

Ingredients:

- 1 cup quinoa, cooked
- 1/2 cucumber, diced
- 1/2 cup cherry tomatoes, halved
- 1/4 red onion, thinly sliced
- 1/4 cup Kalamata olives, sliced
- 1/4 cup feta cheese, crumbled
- 2 tbsp olive oil
- 1 tbsp lemon juice
- 1 tsp oregano
- Salt and pepper to taste

Instructions:

1. In a bowl, combine cooked quinoa, cucumber, tomatoes, onion, olives, and feta.
2. Drizzle with olive oil, lemon juice, and sprinkle with oregano, salt, and pepper.
3. Toss to combine and serve immediately.

Maple Cinnamon Quinoa Granola

Ingredients:

- 2 cups rolled oats
- 1 cup cooked quinoa
- 1/4 cup maple syrup
- 1/4 cup coconut oil, melted
- 1 tsp cinnamon
- 1/4 tsp salt
- 1/2 cup mixed nuts (walnuts, almonds, etc.), chopped
- 1/4 cup dried cranberries

Instructions:

1. Preheat the oven to 180°C (350°F).
2. In a large bowl, combine oats, cooked quinoa, maple syrup, coconut oil, cinnamon, and salt.
3. Spread the mixture on a baking sheet and bake for 15-20 minutes, stirring halfway through.
4. Remove from the oven and mix in nuts and cranberries. Let cool before storing in an airtight container.

Miso Quinoa with Roasted Vegetables

Ingredients:

- 1 cup quinoa, cooked
- 1 cup mixed vegetables (carrots, bell peppers, zucchini), diced
- 1 tbsp olive oil
- 1 tbsp miso paste
- 1 tbsp soy sauce
- 1 tsp sesame oil
- 1/2 tsp ginger, grated
- 1 tbsp sesame seeds (optional)

Instructions:

1. Preheat the oven to 200°C (400°F).
2. Toss vegetables with olive oil, salt, and pepper, and roast on a baking sheet for 20-25 minutes until tender.
3. In a small bowl, whisk together miso paste, soy sauce, sesame oil, and ginger.
4. Combine cooked quinoa and roasted vegetables in a bowl, then drizzle with miso sauce.
5. Top with sesame seeds and serve warm.

Quinoa and Pumpkin Seed Energy Bites

Ingredients:

- 1 cup cooked quinoa
- 1/2 cup oats
- 1/4 cup pumpkin seeds
- 1/4 cup honey or maple syrup
- 1/4 cup almond butter
- 1/2 tsp vanilla extract
- 1/4 tsp cinnamon

Instructions:

1. In a bowl, combine cooked quinoa, oats, pumpkin seeds, honey, almond butter, vanilla, and cinnamon.
2. Mix well and roll the mixture into small balls.
3. Refrigerate for 30 minutes to firm up.
4. Store in an airtight container in the fridge for a quick, healthy snack.

Quinoa and Roasted Apple Crumble

Ingredients:

For the filling:

- 2 apples, peeled and diced
- 1 tbsp honey
- 1/2 tsp cinnamon
- 1/4 tsp nutmeg

For the topping:

- 1/2 cup quinoa, cooked
- 1/4 cup oats
- 1/4 cup almond flour
- 2 tbsp coconut oil, melted
- 1 tbsp maple syrup
- 1/2 tsp vanilla extract

Instructions:

1. Preheat the oven to 180°C (350°F).
2. In a bowl, combine apples, honey, cinnamon, and nutmeg. Place the mixture in a baking dish.
3. In a separate bowl, combine cooked quinoa, oats, almond flour, coconut oil, maple syrup, and vanilla.
4. Sprinkle the topping evenly over the apples.
5. Bake for 25-30 minutes until the topping is golden and the apples are tender. Serve warm with a scoop of vanilla ice cream or yogurt.

www.ingramcontent.com/pod-product-compliance
Lightning Source LLC
LaVergne TN
LVHW061956070526
838199LV00060B/4163